The Clark Family
entering Grade IV

THE WHISTLING TEAKETTLE

and other stories about Hannah

Illustrated by Karen Ann Weinhaus

THE WHISTLING TEAKETTLE

and other stories about Hannah

by Mindy Warshaw Skolsky

Harper & Row, Publishers

New York, Hagerstown, San Francisco, London

FIRST EDITION

Library of Congress Cataloging in Publication Data
Skolsky, Mindy Warshaw.
  The whistling teakettle and other stories about Hannah.

  SUMMARY: Relates the adventures of a young girl growing up in New York City
during the 1930s.
  [1. New York (City)—Fiction.   2.   City and town life—Fiction.   3.   Humorous
stories]   city + town
I. Weinhaus, Karen Ann.   II.   Title.
PZ7.S62836Wh   [Fic]   76–21395
ISBN 0–06–025688–5
ISBN 0–06–025689–3 lib. bdg.

*To the memory of my parents, Mollie and Izzie Warshaw,
and my grandparents, Hannah and Isaac Markowitz,*

and to Bernie, Nina, and Mark,

with love.

THE WHISTLING TEAKETTLE

and other stories about Hannah

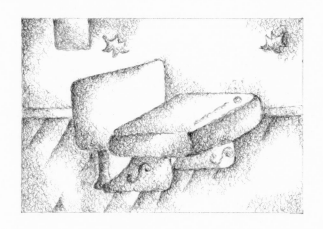

A CHOCOLATE ICE-CREAM CONE

Once there was a girl named Hannah. She lived with her mother and father in a little village between a mountain and a river.

Every autumn, when the leaves on the trees turned colors, the school in Hannah's little village had Parents' Day.

Just before Parents' Day, the teachers hung up all the children's papers that had 100% and neat penmanship. The children were put to work cutting out and hanging up red, yellow, orange and brown paper leaves to make the indoors look like outdoors. Invitations that said "Come see our school" were mailed out to the parents.

But instead of looking at the papers and the leaves, most parents just looked at their own children. None of the children liked that. They got embarrassed. Their faces got redder than the reddest leaves. They looked at the floor and wished they were home.

One year, when it was just about time for Parents' Day, Hannah's teacher, Miss Pepper, made a little speech.

"Please ask all your parents to come to school this year on Parents' Day," said Miss Pepper. "Remember, the class the most parents come to gets a prize. I have never had a class that won the prize. This year I would like to win the prize."

A boy named Willie raised his hand and asked what the prize was.

"I don't know," said Miss Pepper. "It's different every year. Miss Hinckley likes surprises." Miss Hinckley was the principal.

Hannah was surprised that Miss Hinckley liked surprises. At home Hannah's father was always doing things and saying, "Surprise!" But Miss Hinckley and Hannah's father were very different.

"And another thing about Parents' Day," said Miss Pepper, "is that when your parents are here,

4

you must pretend they are not here. You must ignore them. You must act natural."

Then the bell rang.

On the way home, a girl named Priscilla said, "I think the prize last year was pencils."

"Pencils!" said Willie. "It's not worth it. My mother *waved* at me last year! I'd rather write with a crayon!"

Priscilla said, "My father embarrassed me so much last year. He looked at me *like he liked me*, right in front of everybody!"

A girl named Josephine said, "Last year my mother wore a hat that was so big she filled up the whole doorway when she came. I wish she wouldn't come again."

Hannah was glad her mother never wore big hats or waved or did anything to embarrass her. Hannah's mother always looked and acted just right on Parents' Day, and Hannah didn't have to worry about her father because he never came to school for anything because he didn't like to get dressed up.

Hannah told her mother she had been told to ignore her on Parents' Day. Then she asked her mother what "ignore" meant.

5

"It means don't pay any attention to us," said her mother. "But it won't be me you're ignoring. It will be your father. Your father is coming to school on Parents' Day this year."

"Help!" thought Hannah.

When fathers came to school, they wore suits and ties. Hannah's father didn't like suits and ties. He liked plaid shirts with bright colors, like red and blue and green. He liked to smoke cigars. He liked to read newspapers and magazines that told what was happening all around the world.

In fact, he was reading a newspaper and smoking a cigar right then. The pages of the newspaper crackled as he turned them, and blue wisps of smoke came curling up in the air from behind them.

Hannah's mother called the cigars "stinkers." "I hope the smoke from that 'stinker' doesn't kill my new geranium," she said. Hannah's mother loved colors too. She had potted plants all over the house. There were pink and yellow and lavender flowers and bright green leaves with ruffles around the edges on every sunny windowsill.

"We got a letter about Parents' Day in the mail," said Hannah's mother. She took a tiny scissors and snipped a dried leaf off one of her plants.

Hannah asked her father why he was coming to Parents' Day.

"I thought you didn't like to come to school," she said.

Hannah's father looked over the edge of his paper and shrugged his shoulders.

"Your mother talked me into it," he said.

"Otherwise the teacher will think you don't have a father," said Hannah's mother. She watered her new plant with a little sprinkling can she had saved from the days when Hannah had a sandbox. The wet dirt and the green leaves smelled fresh and good to Hannah, just like the outdoors after a rain.

"You come too," said Hannah to her mother. "Miss Pepper said she wants to win the prize for having most parents."

"No, I came all the other times," said Hannah's mother. "I'll stay home and tend to my plants and things. It's your turn this year," she said to the back of Hannah's father's newspaper.

"I think I'll write a letter to the editor," said Hannah's father. He always said that when he read something in the newspapers he didn't agree with.

"I'm sure it will be finished by Parents' Day," said Hannah's mother.

7

When Parents' Day came, all the children were worried.

This time Hannah was more worried.

Miss Pepper's throat was so dry she had to take a cherry cough drop, and then she made another little speech.

"Remember all the rules of good behavior," she said. "Sit up tall, no talking or giggling, and no paper airplanes. And also remember what I told you before: Pretend they are not here. Ignore them. Act natural."

Hannah worried her father might do something she couldn't ignore. Sometimes he did funny things at home that made Hannah laugh. But she didn't want him to do anything that would make the other children laugh at him. So she worried.

Then the parents came.

They came one at a time.

They signed their names in a book.

But they didn't really have to sign their names. Because every time a mother or father came in, a different face got red. That's how you could tell whose mother or father it was. But Miss Pepper wanted the names to see if they could win the prize.

Willie's mother walked in with a big fancy hat

8

like Josephine's mother did last year, and Willie
got a nosebleed.

His mother ran over to his seat and helped him
with his nose!

Hannah worried more. She worried her father

9

would come in with a cigar. She had forgotten to tell him there was no smoking cigars in school.

She worried he would bring a big newspaper and open it up and read it.

She worried he would wear the red and blue and green plaid shirt that looked very nice on a father at home but wouldn't look the same on a father in school. She worried he would forget about a suit and tie.

Hannah's father was the last parent to come.

He didn't do any of the things she worried about.

He did something *worse*!

He walked over to Hannah's desk, he *smiled* and he handed her a chocolate ice-cream cone—*with sprinkles!*

Right in front of the whole class and Miss Pepper!

And he said, "Surprise!"

Priscilla asked Hannah's father to sign the book and showed him where the parents' seats were in the back of the room.

Hannah didn't know what her father did next, because she couldn't take her eyes off the ice-cream cone sticking up out of her hand.

She stared at it until it started to melt.

Then she waved her other hand and pretended

she had to go to the bathroom.

She ran out of the room and into the girls' room with the ice-cream cone.

Nobody else was in there.

She looked at the ice-cream cone some more.

She still didn't know what to do with it.

It was chocolate. Hannah didn't even like chocolate. She liked vanilla. Her father liked chocolate.

She liked sprinkles though.

So she quickly ate off all the sprinkles. Then she got worried. What if Miss Pepper could see through walls! She dropped the ice-cream cone out the window.

Hannah saw the ball of ice cream fall out of the cone and she felt like she was falling out with it.

The ice cream landed on the ground before the cone. It went *plop!* "He brought me his favorite flavor!" she thought all of a sudden. "My father *likes* me!"

Hannah ran back to the classroom and took her seat. Then she turned to where the parents' chairs were to smile at her father so he'd know she liked him back.

But he was gone!

Hannah thought he left because he felt bad that she ran away.

She felt terrible.

It was ten minutes to three. A monitor from Miss Hinckley's office came to collect the books with the parents' names.

At five minutes to three, the monitor from Miss

Hinckley's office came back with the book and a
big bag.

"This class won the prize by one person," said
the monitor from Miss Hinckley's office.

"Well done, class!" said Miss Pepper.

13

"What's the prize?" yelled the children.

Miss Pepper opened the bag and peeked in.

"It's Dixie cups," she said.

"Hooray!" everyone yelled.

They each got a Dixie cup and a little wooden spoon.

The buzzer rang and they all ran out with their Dixie cups.

The Dixie cups were half vanilla and half chocolate. Hannah ate the vanilla half. Then she put the cover on.

She ran home to her house.

Her mother was watering her new geranium with the little sprinkling can.

"Your father certainly got home fast," said Hannah's mother.

"I couldn't wait to get that tie off," said Hannah's father. "It was choking me! I signed the book and came right back."

Hannah looked at her father.

He was wearing his nice plaid shirt. He was reading his newspaper. He was smoking his cigar.

"I like you very much!" said Hannah.

And she gave her father the chocolate side of the Dixie cup.

THE BIG SNOW

One day in the wintertime, a package arrived in the mail; and on the mailing label, in the place where it said TO, it said TO HANNAH, and in the place where it said FROM, it said FROM AUNT BECKY. On a penny postcard attached to the top of the package, it said:

> *Dear Hannah,*
>   *This is to wear on freezing-cold snowy days when a person should bundle up.*
>   *Love,*
>   *Your Aunt Becky*
> *P.S. What should I knit next?*

Hannah's Aunt Becky loved to knit things to bundle people up in. She was always sending Hannah warm woolly things for freezing-cold snowy days. In the closet Hannah had three sweaters, two scarves, four pairs of mittens, two tams and a pair of red pom-poms for the tops of her galoshes. ("So if they get mixed up in school," said Aunt Becky, "everybody would know whose galoshes they are.")

Aunt Becky was a very nice aunt, thought Hannah, but she was a terrible knitter. All the warm woolly things she knitted had lumps and bumps in the places where she made mistakes, and the wool was *so* woolly it itched, but Hannah's mother always said Aunt Becky's knitting needles were filled with love. She also said, "It's the thought that counts."

"Well, aren't you going to open your package?" asked Hannah's mother. Hannah opened it as slowly as she could.

"Isn't that nice," said Hannah's mother. "It's a hat."

"It looks like a knitted candy cane," said Hannah. "It's too long. My head's not long like that. It won't fit me."

"It's a stocking cap," said Hannah's mother.

16

"You're supposed to put it on your head and let the long part hang down. Try it on."

Hannah didn't want to, but she thought of Aunt Becky knitting away with those knitting needles filled with love and that big ball of itchy wool on the floor at her feet. She knew she was Aunt Becky's favorite person in the world next to her dog Poopala-darling, for whom she knitted coats and dog galoshes, so Hannah tried the hat on.

"Very nice," said Hannah's mother.

Hannah looked in the mirror. "Ooh—do I look ugly!" she said. "The stripes are all crooked!"

"It isn't easy to knit red and white stripes like that," said Hannah's mother. "Besides, it's the thought that counts. On a freezing-cold snowy day, a hat like that could come in very handy. And don't forget a thank-you note."

Hannah didn't like to write thank-you notes to Aunt Becky because Aunt Becky *always* asked, *"P.S. What should I knit next?"* Hannah knew it wouldn't be polite to write,

> *Dear Aunt Becky,*
> *Please knit nothing next.*
> *Love,*
> *Hannah*

So Hannah told her mother she had a lot of homework to do, and she went into her room, made up a lot of homework and did it.

The next day it snowed all day and it snowed all night, too, so the day after that, the snow was so high there was no school.

"Hooray!" said Hannah when she found out there was such a big snow. Hannah loved snow.

"I'm going up to my special place at the top of the mountain to play," she said.

"There's too much snow," said Hannah's mother. "It's too cold to even stick your nose out the door. They don't call off school for nothing."

Hannah's father came in to warm up from shoveling the walk. "Is it freezing out!" he said.

"And when your father says freezing, you can imagine how it's *really* freezing," said Hannah's mother. Hannah's father loved fresh air so much he opened all the windows wide even on the coldest days and said, "Cold air is healthy!" Hannah's mother always said he was a fresh-air fiend and lowered the windows and said, "Don't waste heat" and "Oh, my poor little plants!"

"It's too cold to open the windows even one inch today," said Hannah's mother to Hannah's father. "It's too cold for you to go out to play," she said to

Hannah. "You'll freeze your nose off."

But Hannah's father opened the windows anyway, and Hannah still wanted to go out.

"We'll all turn into icicles tonight!" said Hannah's mother. There were no radiators in the bedrooms in Hannah's house, and at night the sheets were icy from all the cold fresh air that came in through the windows Hannah's father kept opening all day. Lots of times her mother slipped a hot-water bottle under Hannah's feather quilt to warm her feet.

"I'll bundle myself up," said Hannah.

"First eat breakfast," said Hannah's mother.

Hannah ate a little stack of pancakes with butter and syrup and then she bundled up.

Over her clothes she put on two of Aunt Becky's lumpy sweaters, her snowsuit, two of Aunt Becky's itchy scarves, two pairs of bumpy mittens, and her galoshes with Aunt Becky's red knitted pom-poms at the top.

Hannah was so bundled up, it was hard to bend over to put on the galoshes.

"Besides being freezing," said her mother, "it'll be very slippery. Your father says the snow is frozen over on the top."

"I'll pretend I'm ice-skating," said Hannah.

19

"Look how bundled up I am with so many things!"

"With everything but a hat," said Hannah's mother. She opened up the closet and took out Aunt Becky's stocking cap.

Before Hannah could open her mouth, her

20

mother said, "On a day like this, who will be out to see you anyway? When they call off school, it's sensible to stay indoors."

Hannah went out and looked around. Everything was high, white and shining. And *cold.* White puffs came out of her mouth when she opened it.

"Look," she said to her father, who came out to shovel the walk some more, "just like smoke rings from your cigar!"

"This is really healthy air!" said Hannah's father through a mouthful of white puffs. "We'll have *some* healthy house to sleep in tonight!"

Hannah climbed over the high snow ahead of the path her father was cutting. There was a layer of ice over the snow and he had to cut through the ice first with the shovel every time he tried to get through to the snow. As Hannah climbed, she heard her father's shovel crunch. She also heard her mother closing the windows her father had opened.

She started up the mountain road to her special place. Usually she ran up the mountain, but not today. The snow was so big and high, and the coat of ice over it was so slippery, that she had to walk very slowly. She felt like an explorer.

21

When she got to the top of the mountain and looked around, everything sparkled with the great, white snow. The ice covered everything and made it shine: the snow, the bark of the trees, the big slopes of snow on both sides of the road going up the mountain.

Hannah went up and down the sides of the slippery slopes, slipping and sliding and laughing.

Then she came to her special place. In the summertime, the special place was hidden by high grass that Hannah had to push through before she could look down, but now it was wide open.

When she looked down at the Hudson River, it was white all the way across. So was the mountain on the other side. The ferryboat couldn't go. Some people were trying to walk or skate on top of the frozen river. They looked like tiny dolls.

"Hellooooo!" Hannah yelled down, even though she knew they were too far away to hear her.

She saw the top of her school and it looked like a gingerbread house with thick white glazed icing on top.

"Hellooooo!" she yelled down to her school too, even though she knew Miss Pepper and the kids weren't in it today.

More white puffs came out of Hannah's mouth when she yelled.

Hannah made believe she was ice-skating. She slid her feet along on the glaze high on top of the hills of snow.

She danced and jumped around to keep warm.

She crunched her galoshes down hard on the ice to see if she could cut through the ice with her feet like her father did with the shovel. The ice made sounds like glass breaking as Hannah cut out footprints through the glaze. She felt like the world had just been born under that ice and snow.

Hannah heard sounds over her head and she looked up. Every branch and every twig was covered with that shiny ice, making a whole mountainful of shining trees with branches clicking together noisily like a hundred Aunt Beckys with knitting needles. Hannah squinted and saw silvery slivers of sunlight shine through the branches. The sky looked bluer and brighter than Hannah ever remembered.

Click, click! went the ice-coated twigs.

Crunch, crunch! went Hannah's galoshes cutting footprints through the ice.

Then all of a sudden something happened.

When Hannah pulled her feet up through the ice, one of the galoshes didn't come up out of the snow with her foot. Neither did the shoe or sock. Or the pom-pom.

Hannah was standing with one bare foot sticking out on the most freezing-cold, snowiest day of the year.

She was so surprised, she just stood on the other foot and stared at the bare one. The bare foot began to turn red like the stripes on Aunt Becky's stocking cap.

"Ow!" yelled Hannah. "My foot's cold. I want my galosh!"

She tried to find it through the opening in the ice, but the snow was too deep and too packed and it was hard to stand on just one foot and try to dig with her hands.

Besides, it was so cold her hands were starting to hurt even through the two pairs of mittens, so she had to stop.

"How'll I ever get home with just one galosh?" thought Hannah.

A minute ago everything had been so nice, and now everything was terrible! Her nose started to run! Her hat fell over one eye. It itched.

Then Hannah got an idea.

She pulled Aunt Becky's long woolly stocking cap off her head and put it on her bare foot!

And she marched down the side of the mountain with a galosh on one foot and Aunt Becky's stock-

ing cap on her other foot.

Her mother came to the door to meet her.

"Why is your hat on your foot?" asked her mother.

"Because I lost my galosh!" said Hannah.

"So come in, quick, and get warm!" said Hannah's mother.

Hannah's father put more coal on the Franklin stove in the kitchen.

They dried the stocking cap on the stove and Hannah's mother brought her a hot-water bottle for her foot.

"You really used your head!" said Hannah's father.

When Hannah had thawed out, she finally wrote a thank-you note to Aunt Becky. It said:

Dear Aunt Becky,

Thank you for the stocking cap. I wore it on a freezing-cold snowy day, and after I wore it on my head, I even wore it on my foot!

Love,
Hannah

P.S. Maybe next you could knit me another stocking cap for my other foot—just in case.

Then Hannah's father opened all the windows again and Hannah's mother closed them, and they all had cups of hot cocoa—with a marshmallow in Hannah's.

When they lifted their cups to drink, Hannah's father said, "Three cheers for Aunt Becky!" and Hannah's mother said, "It's the thought that counts," and Hannah said, "And sometimes thoughts can come in handy!" And she popped the marshmallow into her mouth and licked her fingers.

THE WHISTLING TEAKETTLE

One day in early spring when the pussy willows outside Hannah's windows were like soft gray velvet and yellow-green buds were popping out on all the trees, and birds were flying back from the south and weaving in and out through all the branches, Hannah decided she would like to travel too.

She said to her mother and father, "I think I'm big enough to go to New York City and visit Grandma and Grandpa all by myself."

Her mother called Hannah's grandmother and grandfather on the telephone and Hannah heard her mother say, "Hello, Mama, Hannah would like to come visit you all by herself. Could Papa meet her bus at the bridge?"

And Hannah heard her grandmother say, "Why not?"

So Hannah packed her suitcase and her mother and father walked her to the bus station.

Along the way, they stopped in a store to buy a present for Hannah to take to her grandmother.

Hannah's grandmother never kept presents. Whenever they brought her a present, like the perfume they brought the last time they visited, or the furry bedroom slippers the time before that, Hannah's grandmother said the same thing: "Thank you very much, but it's not a necessity."

Smelling fancy was not a necessity. Furry feet also were not a necessity. Taking the present back seemed to be the only necessity.

"You pick the present this time," said Hannah's mother. "Maybe you can find something Grandma will keep."

Hannah saw a lot of nice things like a shiny necklace and an ivory fan and a tiny purse made of colored glass beads, but she knew her grandmother would say the same to all of those: "not a necessity." Then she saw a bright silver whistling teakettle with a little red bird on the top. "That's just like our new kettle," said Hannah.

"Maybe Grandma would keep that," she thought. "They drink a lot of tea. Their old kettle is so old it has bumps. And this one has a bird that whistles so Grandma won't have to keep going back to the kitchen to see if the water boiled out."

"Maybe this is a necessity," said Hannah. "I pick this."

They paid for it and the shopkeeper put it in a bag.

Then Hannah and her mother and father walked on to the bus station.

When they got there, instead of the three tickets to New York City that they usually bought, they bought just one.

Hannah's mother said, "Now don't forget that Grandpa will meet you on the other side of the George Washington Bridge, and also don't forget to brush your teeth and change your underwear." Hannah's father said, "Don't forget to bring me a piece of Grandma's gefilte fish." Hannah kissed her mother and father good-bye and said, "I won't forget anything but please just don't say those things in front of the bus driver."

Hannah got on the bus and picked a seat by the

window and the driver started the bus. She waved to her mother and father as they looked smaller and smaller, and when they finally looked like two dots in the distance, Hannah turned around and looked at all the nice things ahead of her. The bus driver drove down Broadway and Hannah looked up to see how the branches of the trees on one side arched over and touched the branches on the other side.

"I'm in a tree tunnel," thought Hannah. Then the bus stopped at the corner of Cornelison Avenue and Hannah held her breath and crossed her fingers until she saw which way the driver turned. He went left and Hannah exhaled. The bus was going down to the river road. That was the route Hannah liked best.

"I'm on a bus that goes my favorite way," thought Hannah. "I'm lucky!" And she watched the sun sparkle on the river all the way to the George Washington Bridge.

The George Washington Bridge was new, and when the bus got to the bridge and started over it, Hannah held her breath and crossed her fingers again to make sure the bridge wouldn't crack in half under the weight of all the passengers. (Before the bridge was built, when Hannah and her mother and father had to cross the river on a ferryboat to get to New York City, Hannah used to do the same thing so the ferry wouldn't sink and drown them all.) She held her breath for as long as she could and then she exhaled. It made such a noise, a person in the seat across the aisle looked at her and Hannah slumped down in her seat. She didn't stay that way long, though, because Hannah loved to look all around her when the bus crossed over the George Washington Bridge. It made her feel like she was high in the sky in an airplane. When she looked down, she saw the river and the boats; when she looked up, she saw the cables of the bridge and the sky; when she looked straight ahead, she saw the other end of the bridge. Then she held her breath and crossed her fingers again as she began to watch for her grandfather.

First she saw a dot that grew bigger and bigger as they got closer and closer and then turned into her life-size grandfather just as the bus slowed down.

When she saw him standing there, Hannah felt warm and happy. She exhaled quietly and jumped up, took her suitcase in one hand and the bag with the whistling teakettle in the other hand and got to the front of the bus just as the driver opened the door.

Then Hannah stepped down and landed right in her grandfather's arms.

"Hello, my Hannah from the country!" said Hannah's grandfather, giving her a big hug and a kiss.

"Hello, my grandpa from the city!" said Hannah, giving him a big hug and a kiss right back. "Hey, let me down—your mustache tickles!"

Then he took the suitcase and she kept the bag with the whistling teakettle, and they held hands and walked down the steps to the subway.

They got on a train that said "A," and they rode and rode; then they changed to a train that took them to another train, and they rode and rode some more.

"The subways ride forever," thought Hannah, but finally her grandfather said, "Here we are."

They got out and held hands again and walked up a flight of steps out onto the street.

The street was filled with more people than in Hannah's whole little village in the country. There were tall apartment houses and big stores, medium-sized stores and little stores—so many stores!

"Welcome to the Bronx, New York!" said Hannah's grandfather.

"Grandpa, I *know*," said Hannah. "I've been here before!"

"But never alone," said Hannah's grandfather, and he stopped a lot of people and said, "This is my granddaughter Hannah. She came from the country by herself especially to see us!"

"My grandfather knows all the subways and all the people in New York City!" thought Hannah proudly. Then she saw the little green-and-white-striped awning that she knew was the front of *their* store and she couldn't wait. She ran ahead, opened the door and ran in.

It was the best store in the world. It was a candy store!

Behind the counter, even better than the candy, was Hannah's grandmother. Hannah thought her grandmother was more fun than anybody, even though she made people take back presents. Hannah ran behind the counter and her grandmother ran forward both at the same time.

Then Hannah's grandmother gave her a big hug and a kiss and Hannah gave her a big hug and a kiss right back.

Hannah's grandfather followed her into the store and set her suitcase down.

"Here she is!" he said. He went over to the cash register and took out some change and said, "I'll call and tell them she got here all right so they won't worry."

"Let *me* do it," said Hannah.

Hannah's grandfather opened the phone booth door and put a wooden chair inside. He gave Hannah a dime and two nickels and she climbed onto the chair and put a nickel in the place for nickels. When the operator said, "Number, please," Hannah said, "Nyack 714" and the operator said, "Deposit fifteen cents more, please." Hannah dropped the dime in the place for dimes and another nickel in the place for nickels, and she heard the phone ring. Her mother answered it after just one ring.

"I got here all by myself," said Hannah. "I called all by myself too."

"Wonderful," said Hannah's mother. "Enjoy yourself. And try to eat because it makes Grandma happy."

"Don't forget to bring me home a piece of gefilte fish," Hannah heard her father call.

"Ugh!" said Hannah. Hannah didn't like gefilte fish as the grown-ups did.

"Don't say 'ugh!' to Grandma," said Hannah's mother. "And don't tell her the only thing you like is spaghetti. And try to make Grandma keep the present."

"I will," said Hannah, and then the operator said, "Sorry, your time is up" and Hannah put the receiver down very fast. In Hannah's house and in her grandmother and grandfather's house, when the operator said, "Sorry, your time is up," you put the receiver down immediately even if you were in the middle of a sentence. Otherwise the operator would charge you another nickel. Nobody had nickels to waste in Hannah's house or her grandmother and grandfather's house.

As soon as Hannah stepped down off the chair and her grandfather put it back, Hannah's grandmother said what she always said when Hannah came to visit: "Come into the back room and eat!"

They went into the little room behind the candy store, and before Hannah could even take the whistling teakettle out of the bag, her grandmother had three bowls of chicken soup on the table. There were lots of carrots and noodles mixed in with the big chunks of chicken, and little golden circles floating on the top and steam puffs going up in the air.

Hannah blew on her soup because it was so hot.

While she waited for it to cool, she took the whistling teakettle out of the bag, held it up under the light to catch the silvery shine and said to her grandmother, "This is your present. It's a whistling teakettle!"

"Thank you very much," said her grandmother, "but it's not a necessity."

"But it's a new invention," said Hannah.

"I don't need new inventions," said her grandmother. "Old ones are good enough for me."

"Grandma—your old kettle has bumps."

"But it boils water even with the bumps."

"But sometimes when you're up front in the store, the water boils out."

"So new kettles can't boil out?"

"Not if they're whistling teakettles. The bird whistles and lets you know when the water is boiling. The bird calls you."

Hannah waved the kettle and the bird flashed red in the light.

"Very pretty," said Hannah's grandmother, "but not a necessity."

"Grandma!" said Hannah. She thought of the necklace and the fan and the beaded purse she didn't buy. "I bought this *especially* for being a necessity!"

Just then someone came into the candy store and Hannah's grandmother went out front.

"Grandpa," said Hannah, "can't you make Grandma keep the whistling teakettle? It would make me feel so good if the first time I came by myself I could get Grandma to keep a present!"

"The only present I ever got your grandmother to keep that she said was a necessity was her wedding ring," said Hannah's grandfather. "So I'd like to help you, but I don't think I can. You could show me how that whistling teakettle works, though, because it surely is an unusual thing!" Hannah's grandfather loved new inventions.

"You take the little bird off the top," said Hannah, "and you fill the kettle with water. Then you put the bird back on and light the stove, and when the tea is ready, steam comes out of the bird's beak—just like the steam from Grandma's chicken soup—and the bird whistles and tells you the tea is ready. You don't even have to watch the kettle!"

"Amazing!" said Hannah's grandfather. "With the old kettle, we have to keep running back from the front to look. But what if we were so busy we didn't hear it? The water could boil out then."

"Grandpa," said Hannah, "when that bird whistles, you hear it. Because it whistles louder and louder till you turn it off. You'd hear it even if you were standing outside under the awning!"

Just then Hannah's grandmother called her, so she went out front. Hannah's grandmother was making a malted milk and she knew Hannah liked to watch and say "Now!"

Hannah's grandmother put two scoops of ice cream into a silver container, then a glass of milk, a ladle of chocolate syrup, and a spoon of malted powder. She hooked the container onto the malted machine and the machine made a loud buzzing noise like a bumblebee while the malted went round and round inside the container. When Hannah saw the foam at the top of the container, she said "Now!" and her grandmother took the container off the hook and the malted machine stopped buzzing. Hannah's grandmother poured the malted into a big glass, put the container with the leftover malted next to it and gave it to a boy named Harold who was sitting on a stool on the other side of the counter.

"Hello, Hannah," said Harold's mother. "How's everything in the country?"

"Fine," said Hannah. "Can I make Harold's mother's seltzer?" she asked her grandmother. Hannah knew all the customers and what they ordered, because even though the Bronx, New York, was big, the customers were usually the same ones from the block. Almost every block had its own store. There was one on the next block called Kaplan's that was bigger and fancier and charged higher prices, but Hannah thought her grandparents' store was the best.

While Harold drank his malted with loud slurping noises, Hannah held a little glass under a lever and pulled, and out came seltzer—it looked like water with bubbles—till the glass was full. Then Hannah turned the lever off and gave the glass to Harold's mother. Harold's mother drank quietly. She didn't slurp.

Hannah took a pad and pencil. She copied the prices from a list on the wall:

$$
\begin{array}{lr}
\text{malted} & 15¢ \\
\text{seltzer} & +\ \underline{\ 2¢} \\
\text{altogether} & 17¢
\end{array}
$$

"Isn't she good in arithmetic?" asked Hannah's grandmother.

"She certainly is," said Harold's mother. "Stop that slurping, Harold!" Then she put a dime, a nickel and two pennies down on the counter and said good night.

When Harold and his mother left, Hannah's grandfather came out front. It was his penny-poker night. "See you when I get back," he said. "I'll bring something good from the bakery. And we'll all have tea." He winked at Hannah. "If you put the new kettle on at ten o'clock, I could hear that bird whistling when I come in the door."

"But it's not a necessity," said Hannah's grandmother. "I can boil water in the old kettle and
whistle myself."

"The old kettle is a hundred years old!" said Hannah's grandfather.

44

"So will you be someday, if you're lucky," said Hannah's grandmother.

"Well, I'd like some new tea when I come home tonight just the same," said Hannah's grandfather. "What would you like from the bakery?"

"A charlotte russe!" said Hannah. After penny candy in the store, charlotte russes were the thing Hannah liked best. A charlotte russe was a little sponge cake in a round white cardboard container. It was just big enough for one person, so you got one all your own, and it had whipped cream on the top, and a cherry. They didn't have charlotte russes in the bakery in Hannah's little village in the country. Only in the Bronx, New York.

"Okay," said Hannah's grandfather. "New tea for all of us and a charlotte russe for Hannah when I get back."

When he left, Hannah looked all around her: at the row of round white lights hanging from the ceiling like a bunch of new moons; at the glass jugs of cherries, pineapple, chocolate syrup and walnuts on the counter; at the big candy case filled with boxes and boxes of all kinds of penny candy; at the comic books and movie magazines, pads, pencils and crayons tucked into the shelves that lined the walls.

"Oh, this is the best place in the whole world!" said Hannah, giving her grandmother a hug and whispering, "Keep the whistling teakettle!" in her right ear. Her grandmother hugged her back and whispered, "It's not a necessity!" in Hannah's left ear.

Then her grandmother asked Hannah to tell everything she had learned in school since the last visit, and Hannah did. And Hannah asked her grandmother to tell every movie she had seen in the Bronx since the last visit, and her grandmother did. And Hannah told her grandmother the movies she had seen in the country, and they both did imitations of the actors and actresses.

"Tomorrow I'll make you your spaghetti with the stinky cheese you like," said Hannah's grandmother, "and Grandpa will mind the store and we'll go to the movies together."

"I love to come here!" said Hannah.

She read comic books and movie magazines and helped wait on customers. Then she took a pad and a new box of crayons and drew pictures of everything in the store.

Later, Hannah took an empty sugar cone from a big container under the counter and went over to the candy case. She slid open the doors and slowly picked out her favorite candies. She dropped them into the cone until it was full. She took two licorice sticks, two spearmint leaves, two orange slices, two lemon gumdrops and a candy banana. Two candy bananas wouldn't fit.

A little while before ten o'clock, a lady named Mrs. Beck came in for an ice-cream soda. Most of the customers had the same thing every time, but Mrs. Beck always picked something different. The last time Hannah had visited, Mrs. Beck had ordered a banana split. While Hannah's grandmother was putting the ice cream in Mrs. Beck's glass, she asked Hannah if she'd like some ice cream in her cone.

"After all," said her grandmother, "that's what an ice-cream cone is for."

"I like candy better," said Hannah, drawing Mrs. Beck with a straw in her mouth. "Besides," she said, "it's nearly ten o'clock and I don't want to spoil my appetite." Hannah handed Mrs. Beck her picture and said, "I think I'll put on the tea now." She went into the back room.

"Use the old kettle," called her grandmother.

Hannah sang "My Country 'Tis of Thee" in a loud voice so she wouldn't hear. Then she filled the new kettle with water, lit the stove carefully the way her mother had taught her, put the kettle over the burner and came back out front.

She was still singing "My Country 'Tis of Thee," and Mrs. Beck said she was a nice patriotic girl.

"Ten o'clock," said Hannah to her grandmother. "I'll help you clean up."

"And helpful too," said Mrs. Beck, finishing her soda.

"And an artist?" asked Hannah's grandmother.

"The best," said Mrs. Beck. She said her picture was even better than the last time, when Hannah drew her with the banana in her mouth.

"She takes tap dancing lessons too," said Hannah's grandmother. "I'm going to send a penny postcard to Hollywood and tell them she's better than Shirley Temple."

"Grandma!" said Hannah.

Mrs. Beck said good night and the cleanup began.

Hannah's grandmother washed all the glasses and Hannah pressed each one down on the water sprayer to spray the soapsuds off. They were drying the glasses together when two men walked into the store.

Hannah didn't recognize the men. One of them had a little suitcase. He went into the phone booth.

48

"I'd like a malted," said the other man.

"Closed," said Hannah's grandmother, pointing to the clock.

"Aw, lady," said the man, "please make me a malted. My friend has to use the phone, and I'm dying for a malted. I'll give you a quarter!"

"A quarter!" said Hannah's grandmother. "What are you, a spy from Kaplan's to see if I raised my prices? I charge fifteen cents for malteds." She pointed to the price list on the wall. "My prices are in writing," she said. "The same price for everybody. *I* am not Crooked Kaplan. This is an honest place!"

Hannah's grandmother started to make a malted; and to prove just how honest she was, she made the two scoops of ice cream so big, the malted foamed up to the top before the ice cream was even melted.

Hannah was getting ready to say "Now!" when she noticed her grandmother staring into the mirror behind the malted machine. Her grandmother looked so funny, Hannah looked into the mirror too to see what she was looking at. When she saw, Hannah forgot all about "Now!"

The man in the phone booth was picking on the coin box with a screwdriver and emptying all the coins out. He was stuffing nickels, dimes and quarters into his suitcase.

"It's worse than spies!" said Hannah's grandmother. "It's robbers!"

The man behind the counter reached into his pocket and the malted machine ran over. Hannah's grandmother put her hand on the top of Hannah's head and pushed hard. Hannah landed underneath the counter right in the container of sugar cones. They went "crunch" as she fell in. Her behind was wedged in tight and her legs stuck straight up.

"Grandma!" said Hannah. "Let me up!" Hannah had never seen a robbery except in the movies. Then she got scared maybe the man would shoot her grandmother—like in the movies—so she pulled her grandmother down under the counter next to her.

"What a place for a grandmother," said her grandmother. "I can't fit!"

The malted machine was still buzzing and the malted was running over the counter and down to the floor. It made *slop! slop!* sounds as it landed in front of Hannah and her grandmother.

"E-e-e-e!" A loud screechy noise filled the room. It was so loud it made the buzzing of the malted

machine sound like a little fly instead of a bumble-bee.

"Police whistle!" yelled the man in front of the counter.

"E-e-e-e-e!" It got louder.

Hannah heard loud footsteps running. She heard the phone booth door open, a sound of something dropping, lots of clattering sounds, and more footsteps running.

And "E-E-E-E-E-E!"

"Police! Police!" called Hannah's grandmother, getting up and running toward the front door after the two men.

"E-E-E-E-E-E-E!"

Hannah got out of the box of sugar cones and ran after her grandmother. She slipped on the malted, tripped over the open suitcase, and skidded on a bunch of nickels.

"E-E-E-E-E-E-E-E!"

Hannah's grandfather came running in the front door carrying a little white box.

"What's going on here?" he yelled.

"Police!" called Hannah's grandmother. "We had a robbery!"

"A robbery!" yelled Hannah's grandfather.

"A holdup of the Bell Telephone Company!"

yelled back Hannah's grandmother. "Don't you hear the police whistle?"

"E-E-E-E-E-E-E-E!"

Hannah started to laugh.

"What's the joke?" asked her grandmother.

"It's not a police siren, Grandma," yelled Hannah. "It's the whistling teakettle. *The tea is ready!*"

For a minute nobody said anything. Then Hannah's grandfather turned off the malted machine and Hannah ran to the back room and turned down the burner on the stove and everything got quiet.

After a minute, all three of them began to laugh, and they laughed so hard they had to sit down, and even after they sat down, they still kept laughing.

When they had laughed so much they couldn't laugh anymore, her grandfather mopped up the malted and picked up the nickels. Then they all went into the back room and had a glass of tea with lemon and sugar, and Hannah had a charlotte russe.

Hannah stayed for two days. Her grandmother made her spaghetti with stinky cheese and they went to the movies.

Before she left, she and her grandmother

hugged and kissed each other good-bye and her grandmother gave her gefilte fish for her father. Her grandfather took her on the subway back to the bus on the New York City side of the George Washington Bridge, and she and her grandfather kissed each other good-bye and Hannah got on the bus.

As the bus started back over the bridge, it was just beginning to get dark. Hannah sat by a window so she could wave good-bye to her grandfather. She waved till she couldn't see him anymore and then she looked at things outside.

She looked down at the lights twinkling on the tugboats and up at more lights going on all over the cables of the bridge, and still higher up at the stars just beginning to come out in the sky.

The moon looked like a little lemon gumdrop and Hannah watched it sparkle on the dark shiny Hudson River all the way back along the river road.

Hannah could hardly wait to see her mother and father, who she knew would be waiting for her at the bus station back home in the country.

She couldn't wait to tell them about the robbery.

But she would tell them about the robbery second.

Because first, she would tell them that her grandmother had *kept the whistling teakettle!*

"That little bird on the kettle maybe saved our life!" Hannah's grandmother had said. And life, she said, was a necessity!

SOMETHING LOVELY

Every day after school Hannah's favorite thing to do was to go to the top of the mountain that she lived at the bottom of.

First she changed her clothes. Then she drank a glass of milk. Then she packed a little snack to take along. Then she said hello and good-bye to her mother and father.

And then she started at the bottom of the mountain and ran all the way till she got to the top.

Hannah could run up and down the side of that mountain so fast!

In the autumn, when the colored leaves dried

and fell from the trees, she ran up to her special place at the top and piled the crispy leaves in bunches and jumped in to hear them crunch. In winter she had to go slower but she still liked to get to the top and see how it looked when everything was all covered with white. In spring she ran up to look for violets and wild-strawberry leaves (and one day she found her old galosh she had lost in the snow!). But best of all, she liked the special place at the top of the mountain in summer, because then the grass grew so tall, she had to push her way through to get there, and then the special place was hidden and felt like a secret.

When she walked through the high grass, she held her breath and crossed her fingers to make sure the beautiful view would still be there.

When she got through the tall grass, she came to a clearing where she could see up and down the Hudson River and all the way across to the other side, and she exhaled from holding her breath so long.

Every time Hannah looked at the view, she felt like she was seeing it for the first time. She loved the picture.

All below her were treetops and rooftops, but the best part of the picture was the river itself and the little villages Hannah could pick out from the clusters of dots on the other side. She could fit ten miles up and down that river all in the space of her eye!

Hannah sat right at the edge of the mountain and let her legs dangle over and ate her snack. There was a funny old tree sticking out at an angle from the edge of the mountain and Hannah liked to look at it and try to figure out where each jagged branch was joined to the trunk. Later, when she was home, she tried to draw the funny tree from memory in her drawing book.

She also liked to push at pebbles with her toes and listen as they dropped softly over the edge and made soft muffled sounds through the tops of the trees below.

She liked to be alone like this to just sit and look and think about things.

She watched the river, the ferryboat going across and the other boats going up and down, and she watched the sky and the shapes of clouds. Sometimes the clouds had funny shapes and sometimes they even looked like an animal or a person. Once she saw Peter Rabbit and once she saw her teacher, Miss Pepper!

On one of the first days of summer, when everything was warm and green, Hannah's grandmother and grandfather came out from New York City to visit. They brought big shopping bags filled with boxes and jars of things like gefilte fish for Hannah's mother and father and a charlotte russe especially for Hannah. Hannah was so excited and happy to see her grandparents that she couldn't eat it right away, so the charlotte russe was put into the refrigerator so the whipped cream wouldn't spoil.

Hannah's grandfather said, "I feel tired from the trip and the warm weather," and he took a little nap.

Hannah's mother said to Hannah's grandmother, "Mama, would you like to take a nap too?" But Hannah's grandmother said, "No thanks. Hannah and I will be too busy talking."

Hannah and her grandmother always had a lot to talk about. Hannah looked at her grandmother and thought of all the nice things her grandmother did for her. She thought of the movies they went to see together and the way her grandmother told her the whole stories of all the movies she saw when Hannah wasn't with her. She thought of the way her grandmother always asked about school and what Hannah was doing and how she felt. She thought about the stories her grandmother made up for her, especially the stories about what Hannah called "the olden days" when her grandmother was a girl. She thought of the spaghetti with stinky cheese her grandmother kept in a little cabinet over her stove and made just for Hannah.

"Grandma," said Hannah, "you're my very best friend."

"And you are mine too," said Hannah's grandmother.

They hugged each other.

"And Grandma," said Hannah, "I'm going to show you my special secret place at the top of the mountain that I never showed anybody else in the world!"

"Now?" asked Hannah's grandmother.

"Grandma!" said Hannah. "I thought you'd be glad."

"Don't forget I'm not a young girl anymore," said Hannah's grandmother. "I'm a city person now, not a country one. I'm used to trolley cars and subways and not so much walking. And there are no mountains in the Bronx, New York!"

"But Grandma," said Hannah, "that's just why you should come! Besides, it's not really a mountain; it's just a big hill. You'll see—if you come up with me once, you'll want to come all the time."

"Well, we'll have to walk very slowly," said Hannah's grandmother.

Hannah said she would. She put the white box with her charlotte russe and two cold bottles of soda and four straws into a little basket, and then Hannah and her grandmother started up the mountain road to see Hannah's secret place together.

At first, Hannah remembered about walking slowly. But when they were halfway up the mountain, Hannah began to get excited and couldn't wait to show her grandmother the beautiful view. She started to run.

When she got up to where the high grass was, she turned to tell her grandmother they were almost there, but her grandmother was nowhere to be seen.

So Hannah started running back down the mountain and found her grandmother resting on a big rock halfway down.

"I'm huffing and puffing like the big bad wolf," said Hannah's grandmother. "This may be just a hill to a country girl like you, but to a city grandma like me it's a big mountain. Also it's hot. I have to rest."

Hannah sat next to her grandmother on the big

rock and rested too, but she felt very wiggly.

Finally her grandmother felt rested enough to continue, and Hannah controlled herself and slowly walked the rest of the way up with her.

When they got to the high grass, Hannah said,

"We're almost there!" and started to push through.

When the grass tickled her nose, Hannah turned to her grandmother and said, "You're older so to you it's a mountain and to me it's a hill, but you're also bigger so on you the grass comes just to your waist but on me it comes up to my nose."

"Listen to Albert Einstein!" said Hannah's grandmother and Hannah giggled. Her father always said Albert Einstein was the smartest scientist in the world. He had a book about him and had been on the same page for three years.

When they got through the high grass and came to the clearing, Hannah made a big wide arc with her arms and said, "Look!"

Hannah's grandmother looked for a long time. She didn't say a word.

"Don't you like it?" asked Hannah. "Don't you think it's beautiful?"

Hannah's grandmother was still quiet. Finally she said, "This is really something lovely. Thank you for showing this to me."

"Now let's sit down and have our picnic and look at things and talk," said Hannah. "I always wanted to talk about this place to somebody but this is the first time I ever brought anybody up here. It's such a special place it had to be a special person."

"This is a real compliment," said Hannah's grandmother. "I was never called 'special' before."

"But you call me special all the time, Grandma."

"You are. You are my very special grandchild."

"Well, you are my very special grandmother. And this is my very special place."

They sat down and Hannah took the four straws out of the basket. "Two apiece," she said. "In school at milktime, everybody asks the straw monitor for two straws." She took out the two bottles of soda. Then she looked in the basket and all that was left was the little white box with the charlotte russe in it.

"I forgot the bottle opener!" said Hannah. "I'll be right back!"

Hannah raced all the way down the mountain road and into her kitchen. She said hello to her mother and father, who were having a nibble of the gefilte fish. Her grandfather was still resting.

"What happened?" asked Hannah's mother.

"I forgot the bottle opener."

"You came all the way home for a bottle opener?"

"How else can I open the bottles?"

"This is really good gefilte fish," said Hannah's father.

Hannah said good-bye and ran all the way back up the mountain.

"How is this humanly possible?" asked her grandmother. "I think you are secretly a mountain goat!"

"You're the big bad wolf and I'm a mountain goat," said Hannah. "And now you'll come up here with me every time you visit, won't you?"

"No," said Hannah's grandmother, "I won't be able to do it again."

"Oh, *Grandma!*" said Hannah. "Why not? I thought you'd love it here!"

"I do," said Hannah's grandmother. "I love it even more than you thought I would. While you were gone, I looked and looked and it reminded me of something. I remembered I wasn't always a city grandmother. Once I was a little girl like you and there was just such a special place I used to go to in my little shtetl in Poland a long, long time ago."

"What's a shtetl?" asked Hannah.

"A village," said Hannah's grandmother. "That's how you say it in Jewish."

Hannah knew some Jewish. It was what her mother and father spoke when they didn't want her to understand what they were talking about. She learned all the words she wasn't supposed to understand very fast. Now she knew a new word.

"Tell me about the special place in your little shtetl," said Hannah.

"Well, there were no modern washtubs with washboards like people have now," said Hannah's grandmother. "The people in our shtetl were very poor. My mother used to wash our clothes on the banks of the river, not such a big river as yours, but a little river, more like a brook, and I used to play with the other children whose mothers were washing clothes along with my mother. We used to run and chase each other and fool around and have a lot of fun while our mothers washed the clothes."

"Did the mothers have fun too?"

"For the mothers it was no picnic. My mother had a backache every night after washday. The only fun the mothers had was talking with the other women."

"What did they talk about?"

"They talked about how hard it was to bend down and wash clothes on the banks of the river."

"And what did *you* do?"

"I played with the other children. I ran then like you run now. It was so pretty there I never forgot it. I still remember how the sun was shining on the water. And ever since then I love rivers. So you see

66

I love your view not only once but twice! But I'm too old to climb mountains anymore. I'm too old to even climb hills. Now I've climbed with you and I've seen it and I'll remember it for the rest of my life. While you were gone I took a snapshot inside my head and put it right next to the one of the river in my little shtetl."

Hannah leaned her head against her grandmother's shoulder. "I love to hear stories about the olden days," she said.

"I know," said Hannah's grandmother. "And I enjoy telling them. But the best time of all is the days that are *now*, because now there is you! I liked being a little girl; I liked being the mother of a little girl—"

"*My* mother!" interrupted Hannah.

"That's right," said Hannah's grandmother. "And now I like being the grandmother of my own girl's little girl."

"And that's why I wish you would always come up here with me again," said Hannah.

"Look," said Hannah's grandmother. She pointed to the right. "That way is the Bronx, New York. Whenever you are up here and you look down the river in that direction, you can think of Grandpa and me and maybe at that same minute we'll be thinking about you, because Grandpa and

I think and talk about you a lot. And every time I think about this beautiful view I just snapped the picture of in my head, I'll think of you too, so you'll be in my thoughts even more.

"And don't feel sad that I can't come up here again, because sometimes to share something lovely even once can be enough to last a lifetime.

"Now let's enjoy the time we have while we have it. And let's drink our sodas before they get warm, and you eat your charlotte russe before the whipped cream spoils."

Hannah and her grandmother sat next to each other and drank their sodas through their straws. Hannah took the shiny red cherry off the top of her charlotte russe and looked at the whipped cream.

"The whipped cream looks like one of the clouds," said Hannah. And she ate it. Then she ate the little round sponge cake that was inside the paper container under the whipped cream. Then she ate the cherry. Then she licked her fingers and said, "That was very delicious."

Then Hannah and her grandmother sat close together and looked at the view some more and watched how slowly the boats moved and wondered about the people who were in the boats on the river and in the houses on the mountain on the other side. Then they saw two yellow butterflies.

After that they lay on the ground and talked about how big the sky was and found all kinds of funny shapes in the clouds. They found a wolf and a goat and they even found three that looked like Hannah's mother and father and grandfather.

"Which reminds me," said Hannah's grandmother, "they are probably waiting for us down there."

"Grandpa must be wanting to see me," said Hannah. "Let's go down and tell them they're special too."

"In different ways," said Hannah's grandmother, "every person is special."

"But especially us," thought Hannah. "When we get home, I'm going to make a picture of the river in the little shtetl with the mothers washing clothes and the children playing all around and the sun shining on the water. It will be a surprise for my grandmother."

Then Hannah and her grandmother put the empty bottles and the bottle opener and the cardboard container from the charlotte russe in the little picnic basket and they held hands and walked slowly down the mountain together, enjoying all the beautiful things that were all around them.

Format by Gloria Bressler
Set in 12 pt. Primer
Composed by The Haddon Craftsmen, Scranton, Pa.
Printed by General Offset
Bound by A. Horowitz & Son
HARPER & ROW, PUBLISHERS, INCORPORATED

CHILDREN'S HOSPITAL OF WASHINGTON, D. C.